lettering the Psalms

BEGINNER & INTERMEDIATE CHRISTIAN LETTERING PRACTICE & PROJECTS

Inspired to Grace

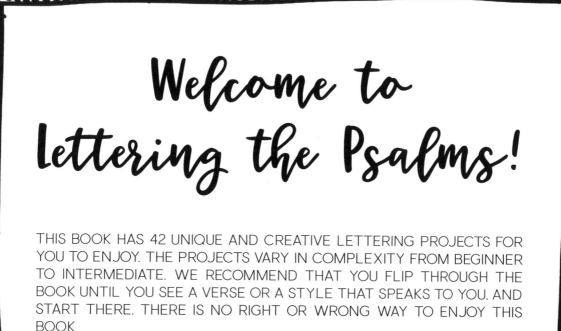

Welcome to Lettering the Psalms!

THIS BOOK HAS 42 UNIQUE AND CREATIVE LETTERING PROJECTS FOR YOU TO ENJOY. THE PROJECTS VARY IN COMPLEXITY FROM BEGINNER TO INTERMEDIATE. WE RECOMMEND THAT YOU FLIP THROUGH THE BOOK UNTIL YOU SEE A VERSE OR A STYLE THAT SPEAKS TO YOU, AND START THERE. THERE IS NO RIGHT OR WRONG WAY TO ENJOY THIS BOOK.

LETTERING THE PSALMS IS PRINTED ON 60-POUND BRIGHT WHITE STOCK WHICH ALLOWS US TO PROVIDE AN EXCELLENT VALUE TO OUR CUSTOMERS. IF YOU HAVE ISSUES WITH BLEEDING, OR IF YOU MAKE A MISTAKE AND WANT TO START OVER, YOUR PURCHASE INCLUDES A DOWNLOAD CODE WHICH WILL ALLOW YOU TO SIGN UP FOR OUR NEWSLETTER AND THEREBY ACCESS ALL THE LETTERING PROJECTS IN THIS BOOK AS PDF DOWNLOADS.

SIGN UP AT: WWW.INSPIREDTOGRACE.COM/LTP

YOUR DOWNLOAD CODE: **LTP2623**

 @inspiredtograce

 Inspired to Grace

be still

KNOW AND
THAT I AM
God

PSALM 46:10

LETTERING PROJECT 2

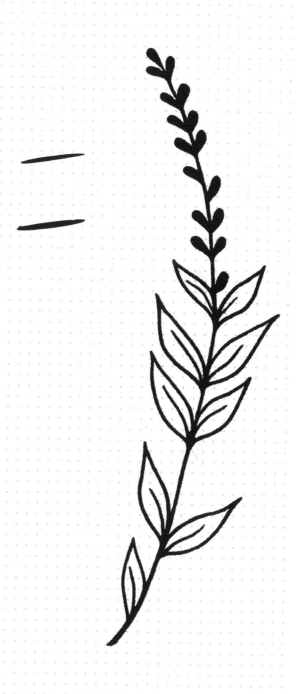

BE STRONG AND TAKE HEART *and* **WAIT FOR THE LORD**

PSALM 27:14

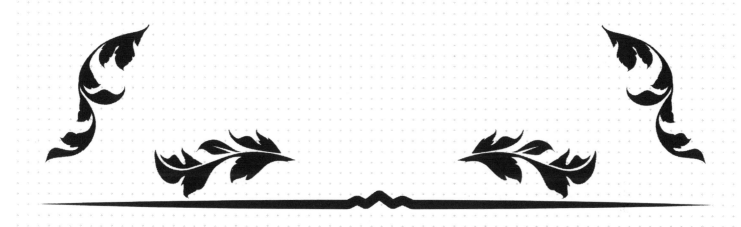

LETTERING PROJECT 3

BLESS THE Lord, O my Soul

PSALM 103:1

Lord

CAST YOUR Burden on the LORD & HE shall Sustain YOU

Psalm 55:22

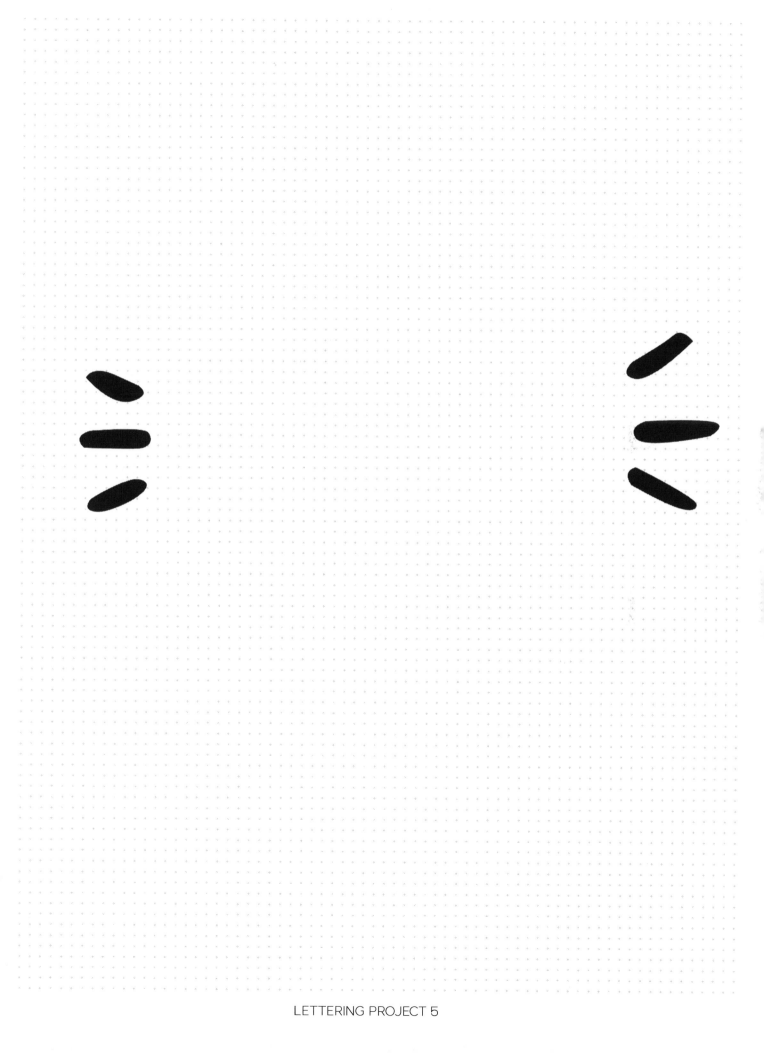

CHILDREN

ARE A GIFT

from the

Lord

PSALM 127:3

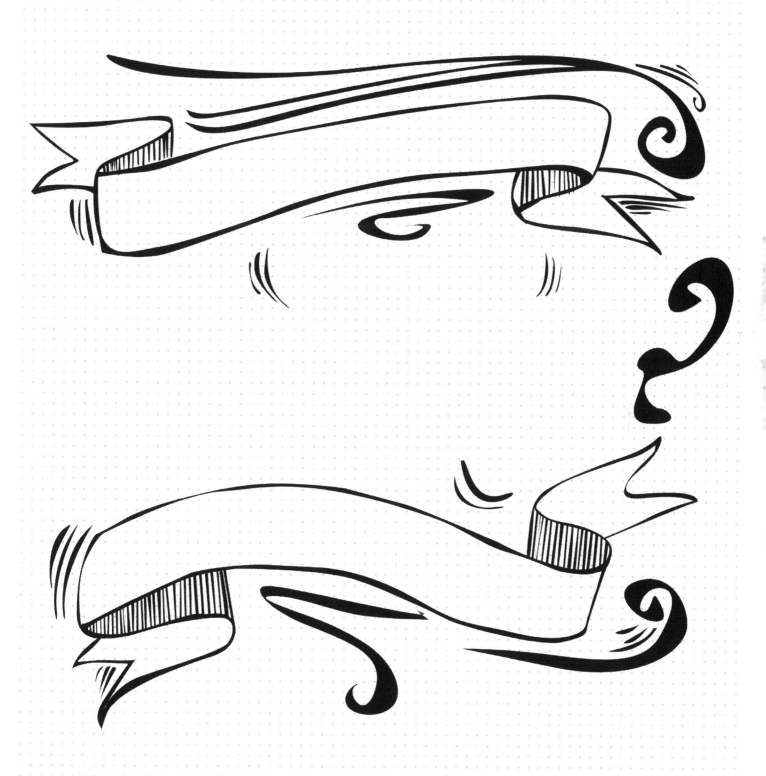

Create
IN ME A
clean heart,
O GOD
PSALM 51:10

Deliver me from my enemies my God

Happy are those who do not follow THE ADVICE OF THE wicked PSALM 1:1

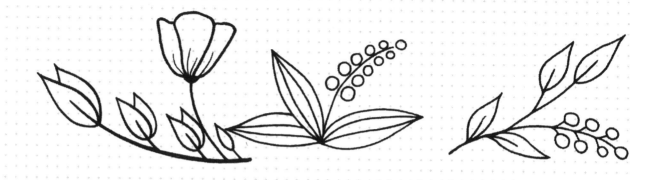

HAVE MERCY ON ME
O GOD
BECAUSE
OF YOUR
unfailing
LOVE
PSALM 51:1

He leads the **HUMBLE**
in what is right and
TEACHES
Way them his
PSALM 25:9

HE WILL Order his Angels to Protect you WHEREVER YOU GO Psalm 91:11

I call on you, my God, for you will answer me; turn your ear to me and hear my prayer Psalm 17:6

I can never

ESCAPE

FROM YOUR

SPIRIT!

PSALM 139:7

I FEAR NO EVIL
for you are with me
PSALM 23:4

LETTERING PROJECT 15

LETTERING PROJECT 15

I LIFT my EYES TOWARD the MOUNTAINS PSALM 121:1

I WILL BLESS THE Lord AT ALL TIMES

PSALM 34:1

LETTERING PROJECT 18

I will sing the name of the

LORD
MOST HIGH

PSALM 7:18

I WILL tell OF ALL YOUR MARVELOUS WORKS

PSALM 9:1

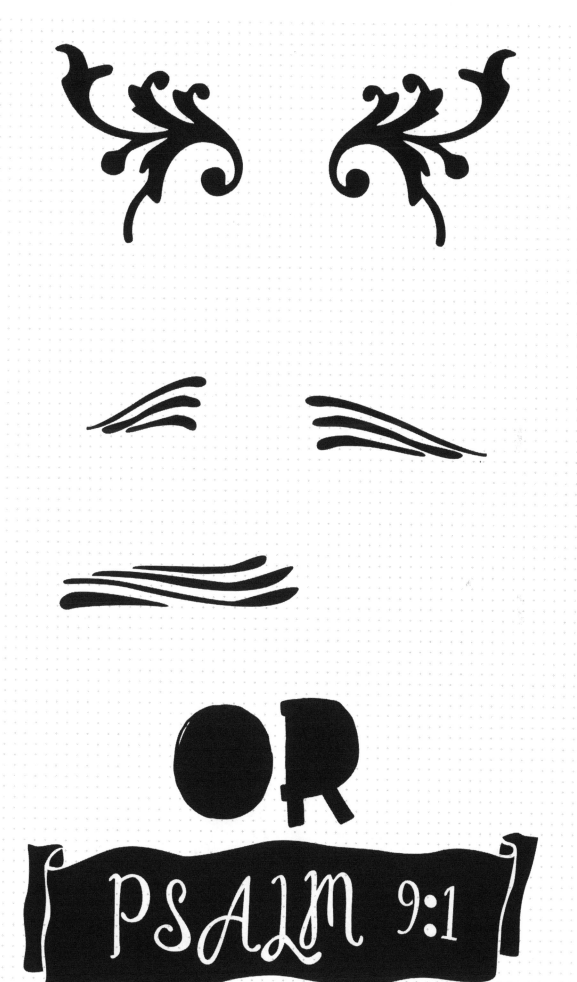

I would rather be a
DOORKEEPER

IN THE HOUSE OF MY
God
THAN DWELL IN THE
TENTS OF THE
WICKED

Psalm 84:10

LET THOSE WHO LOVE THE Lord HATE EVIL Psalm 97:10

LETTERING PROJECT 22

LET US
Break
THEIR
Chains
AND THROW OFF THEIR
Shackles
PSALM 2:3

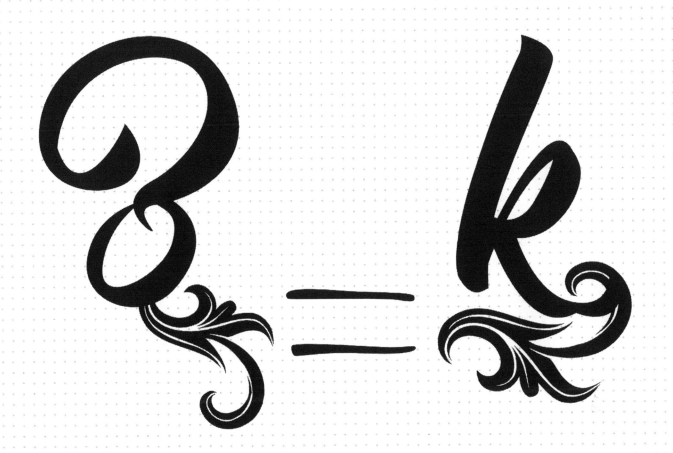

LORD

you

have

SEARCHED

me and known me

PSALM 139:1

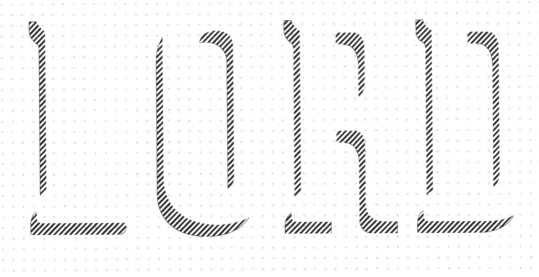

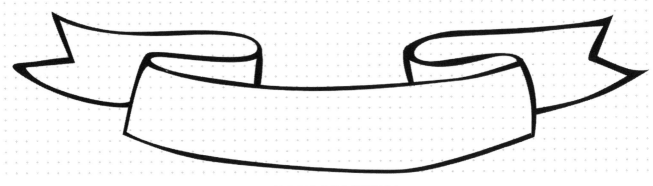

Make your ways known to me, Lord; teach me paths your

··PSALM 25:4··

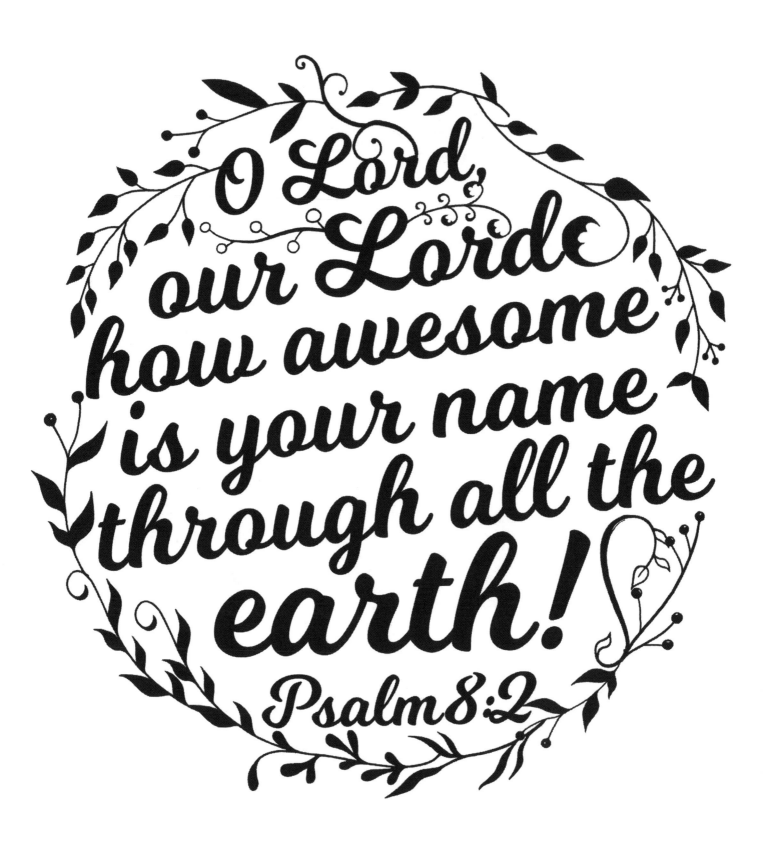

O Lord, our Lord, how awesome is your name through all the earth! Psalm 8:2

O Lord, Lorde

TAKE DELIGHT IN THE

Lord

PSALM 37:4

PSALM 37:4

Taste
AND SEE
that the
LORD
IS GOOD
PSALM 34:8

LETTERING PROJECT 29

THE WORDS OF The LORD are pure WORDS LIKE SILVER TRIED IN A FURNACE OF EARTH PURIFIED SEVEN TIMES PSALM 12:6

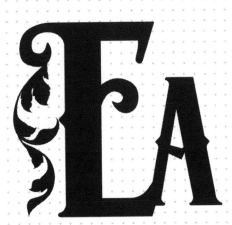

THE LORD is my SHEPHERD I SHALL NOT WANT

PSALM 23:1

THE EARTH AND
everything in it,
the world &
ITS INHABITANTS
BELONG TO THE

LORD

Psalm 24:1

LETTERING PROJECT 32

THE FOOL

says in his

HEART,

"There is no God"

⬛═⬛ PSALM 14:1 ⬛═⬛

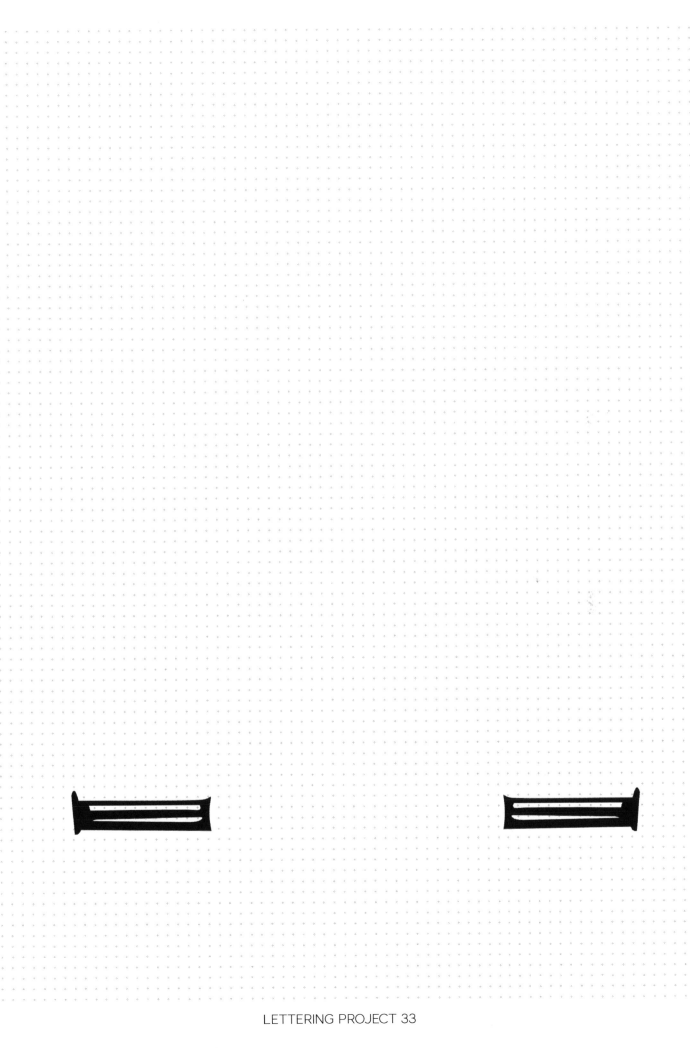

The Heavens declare the Glory of God

Psalm 19:1

LETTERING PROJECT 34

the law of
the LORD is PERFECT
refreshing
THE SOUL
PSALM 19:8

Day
PSALM 118:24

Those who know Your Name will put their trust in you

Psalm 9:10

Thy Word IS A LAMP UNTO MY FEET

PSALM 119:105

PSALM 119:105

The Wicked are not so, but are like Chaff that the Wind drives away PSALM 1:4

YOU ARE NOT A GOD WHO delights in EVIL

PSALM 5:5

You FORMED my INMOST BEING you KNIT me IN MY mother's WOMB

PSALM 139:13

LETTERING PROJECT 41

You will show me the path to life

Psalm 16:11

LETTERING PROJECT 42

BE SURE TO FOLLOW US
ON SOCIAL MEDIA
FOR THE LATEST NEWS,
SNEAK PEEKS, & GIVEAWAYS

inspiredtograce

Inspired-to-Grace

@inspired2grace

ADD YOURSELF TO OUR
MONTHLY NEWSLETTER FOR FREE DIGITAL
DOWNLOADS AND DISCOUNT CODES
www.inspiredtograce.com/newsletter

CHECK OUT OUR OTHER BOOKS!

www.inspiredtograce.com

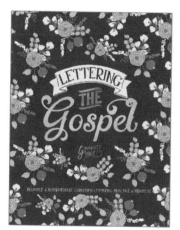

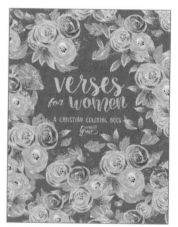

CHECK OUT OUR OTHER BOOKS!

WWW.INSPIREDTOGRACE.COM

CHECK OUT OUR OTHER BOOKS!

WWW.INSPIREDTOGRACE.COM

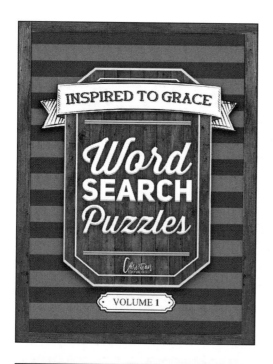

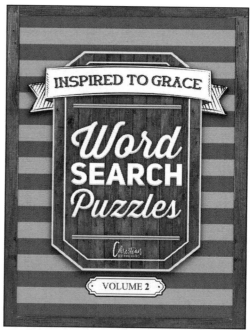

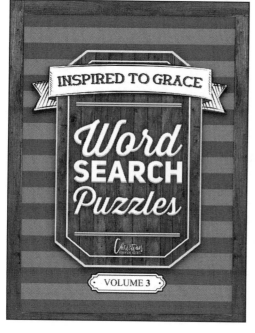

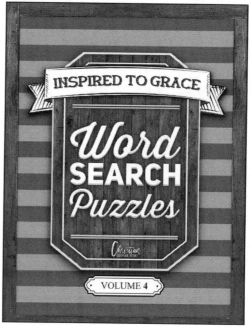

Made in the USA
San Bernardino, CA
04 November 2017